C000133484

FOREWORD

Funny isn't it that since retiring from the track, my recollections consist almost entirely of happy days and fun times! I find it funny because I know only too well how much time I spent training – some mornings even my eyebrows hurt!

I also treasure the memory of that feeling of pure exhilaration on crossing the finish line first, that extraordinary feeling of complete and utter emotional elation, which in its purest form is short lived.

These stars of Welsh sport have all experienced that emotion, and for myself, to have had the pleasure of seeing or remembering their moments in time has been inspirational.

Is it possible to capture in words what it takes to win? Well, Nicole Cooke once told me once how she was always glad to have huge crowds towards the end of the most terrifying hill stages, because the noise of their cheering meant she could no longer hear her own painful, desperate gasps for oxygen as she battled for the finish line and the pure elation of victory.

I think her picture holds true – to win you have to give it absolutely everything.

Colin Jackson

With Doug Smith, manager of the 1971 British Lions in New Zealand.

GARETH EDWARDS

In these days of professional rugby, as interested seemingly in six-figure fees as it is in sublime football, I wonder whether there is enough money to finance the franchise that could put on the field the fifteen best players ever to have played the game? One thing I do know, however, is that there would be no shortage of armchair selectors eager to pick such a team – and they wouldn't have to invest a single penny!

Most positions would be the cause of heated debate. Would it be JPR Williams, Serge Blanco or George Nepia at full back? Bleddyn Williams, Philippe Sella and Brian O'Driscoll might contest the centre positions whilst Gerald Davies, David Campese and Jonah Lomu would fight for the two wing spots. The outside half berth would be hotly disputed – would it be Barry John, Daniel Carter, or Phil Bennett? And such would be the soul-searching selectorial headaches throughout the team.

One thing, however, is sure. There would be no contest when it came to choosing the scrum half. The No. 9 shirt would automatically go to Gareth Owen Edwards of Gwaun-cae-gurwen.

In an article in *The Independent*, Australia's cricket coach, John

Buchanan paid tribute to Shane Warne: 'Greats in any walk of life are defined by their ability to achieve things beyond others. They do this by skill – technical, physical, mental and tactical.' It is an equally fitting assessment of Gareth Edwards's long and illustrious international career. Perfection in sport is nigh on impossible. Sufficient ambition, dedication and expertise can, however, make excellence attainable and sustainable. Gareth Edwards managed to play the game (and win) with a degree of flair, finesse, strength and panache and for that we are all eternally grateful.

What was the secret of his success – what made him stand out from all the other players who have played in this position? It would take more than the space allocated for this piece to answer such a question. Physically he was strong, his upper body strenth superhuman and his athletic prowess such that he was lightning quick over the first few metres and just as threatening over longer distances. His long, menacing strides allowed him to break tackles with ease and his very presence proved a threat and a menace to opposing defences.

In an era when youngsters play competitive sports at the tender age of six years, and anyone who shows signs of a budding talent is hailed as the next Barry John, Ryan Giggs or Ian Botham, it is interesting to see how Gareth's early years were spent in preparation for the future. Under the guidance of his mentor Bill Samuel, he was encouraged to learn to play many sports. Importance was placed on perfecting skills, enjoying experiences and quietly preparing himself physically and mentally for the challenges ahead.

Thousands of words have been written by many eminent authors on the exploits of this wizard of the rugby field. Many have hailed individual performances for Cardiff, Wales and the Barbarians as his crowning glory. For me, personally, however, one game stands out above all others. It took place in Wellington on July 31st, 1971 and was the third test match in the series played betwen the British Lions and New Zealand on that historic tour. It had been a particularly taxing few weeks for Gareth – a hamstring injury plus several other minor muscular

injuries had plagued him during the early part of the tour. He had been replaced after seven minutes of the first test, the team had been comprehensively defeated in the second test and by this time, Gareth, more than anyone, was acutely aware of the pressure on the team and himself for the crucial third test. There had been many tours of New Zealand by a British Lions team, but they had never won a series in the Land of the White Cloud.

He had now recovered fully from his injury and was out to prove to the New Zealand public that he was a force to be reckoned with. As the players ran onto the field, Gareth resembled a coiled spring, his body language serving notice of the role he was about to play. From the kick-off he was darting this way and that, stalking his opponent around the base of the scrum and causing mayhem amongst the opposition. The rest of the team took their cue from the scrum half and it was obvious to everyone that the Lions were ready to pounce.

The captain, John Dawes, having won the toss had decided to play into the wind. Within five minutes Barry John had opened the scoring with a smartly taken dropped goal. This was closely

followed by a try from the mercurial Gerald Davies, engineered by Gareth who was in devastating form and causing considerable concern to a hallucinated defence. Shortly after the restart, the Lions worked their way into the All Blacks 22 and prepared to attack from a line-out. The ball was deflected to Gareth Edwards who dynamically set off towards the New Zealand fly half, Bob Burgess. A hand-off which could have upended an elephant disposed of Burgess and within the blink of an eye, Barry John had scored underneath the posts. Within thirteen minutes of the match the British Lions were thirteen points ahead. The home side were stunned into submission; Sid Going was under constant pressure and the home side uncharacteristically unsettled. The Lions won the match 13-3, a historic win brought about by careful planning, using the best available materials and utilising the services of the architect in Gareth Edwards.

The final word on Gareth to Max Boyce, Glyn-neath's favourite son, who forged a living thanks to Welsh rugby heroes. It was the day of the England-Wales rugby international in 1978 at Twickenham and Gareth's fiftieth cap. A Welsh supporter who was without a ticket was standing outside the ground in the pouring rain. He called up to some English supporters inside the ground, 'What's happening? What's happening?' and was ungraciously told that all the Welsh team with the exception of Gareth Edwards had been carried off injured. Some five minutes later there came a great roar from the crowd and the Welsh supporter called out again, 'What happened, what happened? Gareth scored, has he?'

And finally! An incident included in Frank Keating's wonderful book, *Up and Under*. Just before the Wales-England international at Cardiff in 1975, the world-renowned scrum half was summoned to Buckingham Palace to receive his MBE. There was a cartoon in the *South Wales Echo* by one of Gareth's great friends, the late Gren Jones, showing two colliers reading the headline 'QUEEN SEES GARETH AT PALACE'. The caption read 'Amazing the lengths some people go to, to try and get a ticket.'

Gareth the Barbarian.

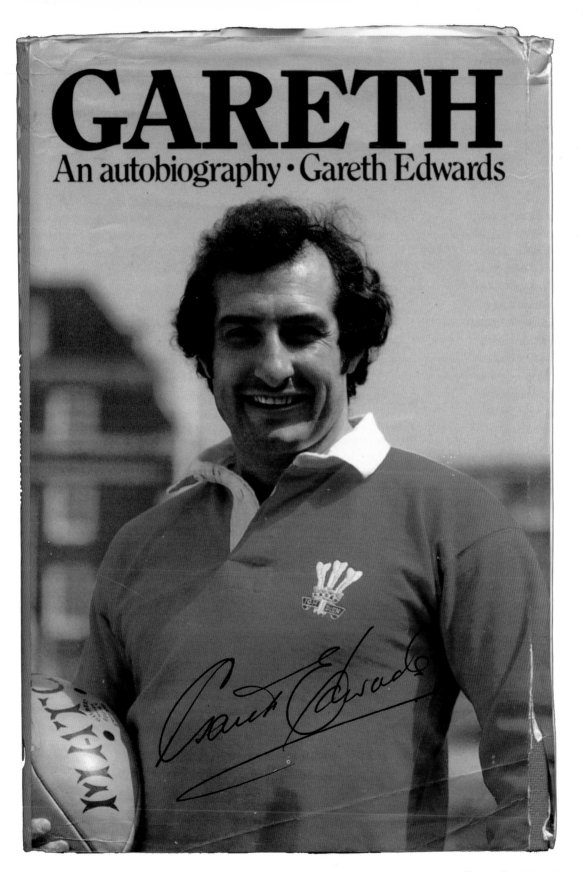

GARETH

An autobiography · Gareth Edwards

Will he kick, will he run, will he pass?

BARRY JOHN

Nijinsky, Michelangelo, Muhammad Ali, Galileo Galilei, Edmund Hillary, William Shakespeare, Johan Cruyff, The Great Wall of China, Enrico Caruso, Aristotle, Joan of Arc, Phidippides, Christopher Columbus, Nelson Mandela, William Blake, Pablo Picasso, Frank Lloyd Wright, the Beatles, Leonardo da Vinci, Mount Everest, James Joyce, Wolfgang Amadeus Mozart, Barry John.

This auspicious list was the winning entry in a competition held by *The Observer* during the late 1990s. The task was to write not more than a hundred words on a sporting hero. The winner was one James Davy of Auckland, New Zealand.

Rugby supporters worldwide associate Barry John with Cardiff Rugby Football Club. This is where the foundations were laid for his legendary partnership with Gareth Edwards and where he spent most of his career. However, it was in the scarlet jersey of Llanelli that Barry first played premier club rugby, and like many a famous player before him, he made his debut while still a pupil at Gwendraeth Grammar School.

His slight physical frame belied his enormous talent. He possessed the consummate artistry and single-mindedness associated with the true greats. Added to this was a gritty determination born of his upbringing in the coal-mining community of Cefneithin. All in all, here was a genius, and this was never better demonstrated than when he scored what he himself considers his finest try. It was for Wales in a Grand-Slam decider against France at Stade Colombes in 1971. Jeff Young, the Welsh hooker, unexpectedly took a strike against the head in front of the French posts. The ball shot back to the outside half who spotted a critical gap between Berot and Bertranne in the French defence. They seriously underestimated Barry's speed and quick as a flash he was over the try-line. Wales went on to win the match and, with it, the Grand Slam for the first time since 1952.

No one has ever had a keener awareness of the opposition's jugular than Barry John. This was admirably demonstrated during the British Lions tour of New Zealand in 1971. The All Blacks were much the stronger team in the first test match but were unable to make inroads into the Lions' territory thanks to a masterly display of tactical kicking from the Lions No. 10. John Reason and Carwyn James take up the story in *The World of Rugby*:

He pulled McCormick, the New Zealand full back, from one side of the field to the other with a string of merciless kicks that almost cut the lines.

McCormick in fact did incredibly well to get as close to them as he did. It was a miracle of positioning and running for him to be able to get near enough to the kicks to stoop and reach for them, but they were almost always just out of his reach, and as he slithered and fumbled, he looked like a player who had come to the end of the international road.

The Lions went on to win the match and the series – a record still unsurpassed in the modern game. To all in New Zealand thereafter, he was 'The King'.

Barry's individual try on that 1971 tour against New Zealand Universities was simply unbelievable. He received the ball from a scrummage just outside the oppostion 22 and in front of the posts. He stood still for a split second and then feinted to drop for goal. The opposition approached, moving in as if to charge down the effort. However, Barry glided past the defenders, moving towards his two centres, Dawes and Gibson. He showed the ball to the next defender, came off his left foot, leaving others standing as if caught in a time warp. Frank Keating describes in his book *The Great Number Tens* how the crowd was stunned into silence as BJ 'tiptoed delicately' underneath the posts. Keating also quotes Carwyn James on the subject:

Instinct, intuition, call it what you like, and a player can be nervous in the extreme at the precise moment, or ice cold and calculating, but suddenly, unpractised, an almost 'accidental profundity' can invade his mind in a split-atom fraction of a second and he will do something he had never thought himself capable of had he planned it for a century.

With two other great Welsh outside halves, Barry John and Jonathan Davies.

PHIL BENNETT

There is a word in Spanish which is used when all other superlatives are inadequate. *Duende* has no equivalent in English or Welsh but it is an adjective which accurately describes that doyen of Welsh rugby, Phil (or Philip, as his wife Pat likes to call him) Bennett.

Duende might also describe Cliff, Bleddyn, Barry, Gerald, Gareth, Ieuan, Jonathan and Shane – that elite group of players who, like the great Welsh poets, can be identified solely by their Christian names. But for all their genius, it is Phil, the Llanelli, Wales and British Lions outside half, that many would place at the head of this group.

All over the rugby-playing world, in clubhouses and bars, there is always a debate raging regarding the respective strengths and weaknesses of the best players, past and present. Inevitably, the hottest subject under review is the outside-half position, and in Wales, we have over the years been proud of those players who have donned our No 10 shirt. But choosing the best is, for me, a straightforward task.

I first saw Phil's genius at work during the 1960s at the

Llanelli Schools' Sevens at Stradey Park. He was playing in the Under 15 section representing Coleshill School. I was sitting in the main stand and eagerly anticipating the next match involving my Amman Valley Grammar School. What happened before my very eyes in the following moments left me, and the few thousand spectators present, completely spellbound. The young lad put on a display of breathtaking audacity which left us all mesmerised – the sidesteps, the ghostly running at incredible pace were all in evidence.

There were, over the years, to be several cameo performances about which to enthuse. One scene is the second test match at Pretoria in 1974. The British Lions outside half took full advantage of ground conditions and ran like an Olympic athlete towards the South African try-line. His sidestepping moves to avoid the opposing defence would have made Torvill and Dean proud. Indeed it seemed as if the graceful Mr Bennett was himself skating along on ice leaving all and sundry prostrate in his wake.

The try scored by Gareth Edwards at Cardiff in 1973, when the Barbarians took on the mighty All Blacks, will go down as one of the finest tries ever scored. Edwards, Quinnell, David, Dawes, Pullin and JPR were all involved in the movement of the millennia. But who was it who got the ball rolling as it were? It was the maestro from Felinfoel. He took possession running backwards and, under enormous pressure, decided to attack. The rest, as they say, is history.

Another much-talked-of try is the one scored against Scotland at Murrayfield in 1977. This was truly a team effort (instigated by Gerald Davies) with Phil again causing mayhem in the Scottish defence before launching himself over the try-line right underneath the uprights.

Indeed, 1977 promised to be a good year for Phil. He was awarded the ultimate accolade of captaining the British and Irish Lions on their New Zealand tour. However, the tour proved an unhappy one, as the Lions backs were unable to capitalise on their forwards' domination of their All Black counterparts. In atrocious weather conditions, the dream became a nightmare and the Lions narrowly lost the series. Consequently, Phil came in for a great deal of unjust criticism from supporters and press alike.

However, once back on home soil, Phil regained his composure and confidence. He was helped by his close friends and many hours representing Felinfoel on the cricket field. The following season saw him leading Wales to a Grand Slam, the final hurdle of which was the home game against France. With the *Tricolores* leading by 7-0, the outside half took matters into his own hands by scoring a try in the corner. This was soon followed by a second try when he took advantage of an inside pass from club colleague, J.J. Williams.

At the end of the season, it was announced that this was to be the last international for both Gareth Edwards and Phil Bennett. What a way to bow out from the game at its highest level.

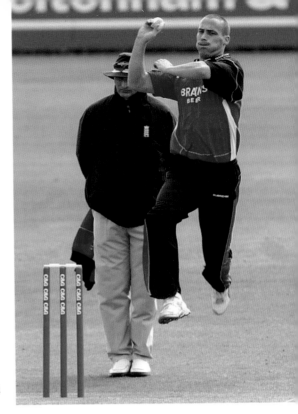

SIMON JONES

The Ashes Test Series is to cricket what the World Cup is to football and rugby. In Simon Jones, therefore, Wales has a world-cup winner. Indeed, during the hotly-contested England-Australia series of 2005, he was arguably the player who made the difference – taking valuable wickets at just the right moment and pinning the batsmen to the crease when it was imperative they score.

His photograph has recently graced the pages of many a glossy magazine, and his face has become as familiar as that of Frédéric Michalak, Gavin Henson, Thierry Henry, David Ginola and Roger Federer – all now associated with modelling agencies and used to endorse a variety of products. His good looks, toned torso, engaging personality and success in the sporting field combine to make him a marketing executive's dream.

But in our obsession with the glittering successes of today, are we in danger of forgetting the achievements of yesterday's men? Wales has, after all, produced any number of cracking cricketers since the legendary W.G. Grace led out an XI to play against the Men of Cadoxton at the Gnoll in Neath. What of Norman Riches, Cyril Walters, Maurice Turnbull, Johnny Clay, Dai and Emrys Davies, Wilfred Wooller, Gilbert Parkhouse, Jim Pressdee, Peter Walker, Jeff Jones, Tony Lewis, Eifion Jones, Tony Cordle, Malcolm Nash, Steve Watkin, Matthew Maynard, Huw Morris, Steve James, Robert Croft, Adrian Dale and Anthony Cottey?

My personal favourites, however, are Glamorgan's Don Shepherd and Alan Jones – the former, a wily spin bowler, and the latter, an elegant opening batsman. Whenever I reflect on the careers of these two players, I despair at the opportunities that were lost to them on the international stage – Alan Jones (34,056 runs on uncovered pitches) and Don Shepherd (2,174 wickets). Alan had a near perfect technique; he was a natural, fluid batsman who played his text-book strokes stylishly. Don's off-breaks made the batsman ponder, often prompting confusion and panic as he enticed them down the pitch

But Simon Jones, the fast bowler from Dafen, Llanelli, who also plays for Glamorgan, seems set to surpass them all.

Another one of the Joneses, Alan this time.

His father, Jeff, played fifteen times for England during the 1960s, taking 34 test wickets. To see Jeff hurtling towards the crease from the Pavilion End at St Helen's was a truly exhilarating experience. He was poetry in motion – the spectators' heartbeats seemed to increase with each pace as he accelerated towards the wicket. One had to feel some sympathy for the poor batsman, as the only defence he had against the red, leather missile firing towards him was the delicately-crafted piece of willow in his trembling hands!

Playing international cricket at Lord's, Headingley, the MCG and the Gabba is the stuff of dreams – and both Jeff and Simon have realised this ambition. Jones senior took six wickets against Australia at the Adelaide Oval in 1966; Simpson, Thomas, Veivers, Burge, Stackpole and Ian Chappell all beaten by his pace. This achievement was emulated by Jones junior during the third test at Old Trafford in 2005 when he took 6-53; Ponting, Gilchrist, Warne, Clarke, Gillespie and Lee all succumbed to the blistering pace and deception of the Welshman's bowling.

Matthew Maynard, another Glamorgan great.

High-quality fast bowlers are as rare as red squirrels and Simon has latterly shown himself to be one of the best. But his success is even mor astounding considering what happened at the Gabba in Brisbane during the 2003 Ashes series. He turned awkwardly while chasing a ball and suffered a knee injury which would have ended the career of many a bowler. Whilst being stretchered off the field, the catcalls and comments from a section of the crowd only hardened his resolve to return and beat the Aussies at their own game. Revenge was very sweet, therefore, come the summer of 2005. Unfortunately, more setbacks kept him on the sidelines for the greater part of the 2006 season resulting in a complete whitewash for Andrew Flintoff's men in Australia.

So what of the future? The Welshman has set his hopes on a full recovery from his injuries in 2008 and then he can have another crack at those Aussies. The whole of Wales will be behind him; I'm not so sure about cricket followers in Wagga Wagga!

Dismissing Adam Gilchrist in the 2005 Ashes series.

NICOLE COOKE

And tell me who she is, again.' Such was the heading above an article by Jamie Jackson in the December 2006 edition of the excellent 'Observer Sport Monthly'. The subject of the article was Nicole Cooke, the first cyclist – female or male – from Britain ever to top the world rankings; the winner of the Tour de France Feminine, the British Road Race Chapionships and the World Cup Series in 2006!

In an increasingly politically-correct society where everything and everyone is given an equal opportunity, it appears that in the realms of sport, testosterone still reigns supreme. It says a great deal about the media and press coverage of several sports – and women's events in particular – that the nation was not aware that we had a world champion in our midst. In a country where winning anything of note is such an unusual occurrence that it gives cause for a national celebration then something is amiss. It is inconceivable that the Australian press would have ignored the success enjoyed by Cathy Freeman or that there would be no column inches or airtime devoted to the Williams sisters in the United States.

On a personal level, I too have to hold up my hand and admit to ignorance when it comes to cycling. As one who likes to think himself possessed of a comprehensive knowledge of sport, I find myself sadly lacking in this genre.

When our children were young and needed entertaining on long journeys, we used to play a game. One of us would think of a name and the others would have to work out his or her identity. You were allowed to ask twenty questions and each answer would be a 'yes' or 'no'. The questions would be as follows :

'Male?'
'No!'
'Olympic Sport?'
'Yes!'
'Is there a ball involved?'
'No!'

During the late 1970s, whilst returning home from Twickenham after yet another victory against England, our car decided to while away the time playing this game. After the twentieth question had not yielded the correct answer, we had to admit defeat. The identity of the sportsman had been chosen by Ieuan Evans, the former Llanelli and Swansea rugby coach, and he was taken aback at our ignorance – we could not identify the sport let alone the individual! 'Good heavens boys. I thought you knew your sport – haven't you heard of Reg Harris, the cyclist?' Here again was a world champion and Olympic silver medallist who was revered more on the continent than in his own country.

To this day, the popular press does not give adequate coverage to women's sport. It is usually tucked in somewhere between the horse racing, crosswords and Sudoku. Women's contribution is often belittled and lambasted by sporting devotees. Then, once a woman goes beyond a certain point, there is a realisation that the individual concerned deserves some column inches. This was the case with Paula Radcliffe, and thankfully, at last, Nicole Cooke is now also beginning to benefit.

In the last year some recognition of her achievements has come her way in the shape of the BBC Sports Personality of the Year Awards, where Nicole was amongst the top six nominees. This was no mean feat when there is still a great disparity between the men and women's events in cycling. Whereas the men are given the chance to attend language courses before competing abroad, stay in the best accommodation and have a back-up team to support them, the women often have to go it alone. After one stage of the Tour de France Feminine in 2006, Nicole found herself sleeping in a tent!

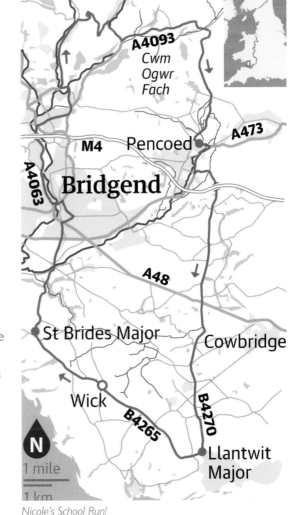

Nicole's School Run!

Choosing the men and women to be featured in this compilation was not an easy task. There were many sleepless nights spent adding names only to then remove them at a later date. However, there was one name that remained constant: Nicole Cooke.

As we are living in an era when we are constantly urged to consider the planet and limit our carbon footprints, the Cooke family from Wick in the Vale of Glamorgan have been way ahead of the times. You would not see them as part of a daily convoy of 'Chelsea Tractors' delivering children to the gates of schools up and down the country. For four years, come rain or shine, Tony Cooke (a physics teacher at Bryntirion Comprehensive School, Bridgend), accompanied by his children Craig and Nicole, could be seen making the journey back and forth from home to school on their bicycles.

The trek which started promptly at 7.20am would follow a carefully planned route from Wick to St Bride's Major. A climb up a steep hill would take them to Heol-y-Mynydd; it was then downhill as far as Southerndown. Sometimes, a ferocious gale would blow in from the Atlantic causing the cyclists to bend over on a 45-degree trajectory to overcome the elements. Once this was achieved there followed a true test of the lung capacity – a perpendicular climb to Norton, down again to Ogmore-by-sea and then a sprint towards the old Volvo garage at Ewenny. This daily ritual usually took the trio an hour to complete, which gave them enough time to shower and change before lessons began.

Nicole's father has been an ever-present influence. Cycling to some extent was in the blood but Channel Four's decision to broadcast the Tour de France in the early 1990s was crucial to her perception of the sport. With her father's promptings and an opportunity to witness at first hand some stages from the Kelloggs Tour of Britain, it was inevitable that Nicole embarked on a career in cycling.

Nicole is a cycle road racer not to be cofused with the cycle track racers of those state of the art velodromes. It's a complex sport, multi-dimensional and the love of Nicole's life. Track racing doesn't appeal to her. From the journalists' point of view the following takes precedence – international male, national male, club male and then occasionally a partial reference to what the women have accomplished. On one occasion, the Cooke family were absolutely flabbergasted when Craig was complimented in a national newspaper for winning a local club event but Nicole's World Cup success wasn't worth a mention. That sums up the prejudice women's cycling has to endure.

Athens 2004.

Being interviewed at the BBC Sports Personality of the Year ceremony in 2006.

Recently, Nicole had this to say to *The Independent*'s Alasdair Fotheringham : 'I have to ride my bike for anything up to 35 hours a week just as training, let alone racing, and do around 23,000 kms of riding a year. Living abroad in Switzerland is an obligation because it's where all the racing and teams are. So dedication in cycling goes without saying, and as a consequence the hardest single thing to take as a professional is unfounded criticism. Some people don't appreciate the degree of dedication cycling takes, and then they criticise you. It really makes me angry.'

I asked Nicole about more positive things, however. What, for instance, was her most memorable race to date : 'Most certainly the Tour de France Feminine. Stage races leave a much bigger impact because they take place over days and days. It's about managing the tired feelings day after day but always remembering that even though in the lead it could only take one mistake to lose everything.'

Physically challenging; mentally demanding. What thoughts emerge from the sub-conscious whilst embarking on a gruelling mountain climb? Nicole again: 'The rhythm of my breathing and trying to count up or down the kilometres depending if I'm nearer the bottom or the top.'

During the early part of the 1990s, a production crew was filming *Rebecca's Daughters* in the Brecon Beacons area. In the make-up room was Peter O'Toole (the man nominated for an Oscar on seven occasions but who has, to date, lost out every time.) Whilst sitting in his chair, O'Toole heard a familiar voice. In an instant he was on his feet and embracing the former Welsh rugby international from west Wales, Ray Gravell. His fellow actors were slightly bemused by his actions, but the Irishman was a rugby fanatic and Gravell was his hero.

How nice it would be, if in the years to come, Nicole Cooke would have the same effect on an equally fanatical follower of her sport. It is to be hoped that once her racing days are over, Nicole be appointed by either the Wales Assembly Government or the Welsh Sports Council to raise the profile of cycling in particular and women's sport in general up and down the land. Hopefully, these bodies will have the foresight and common sense to utilise the example set by this engaging young woman for the good of the nation's sport.

IVOR ALLCHURCH

Phil Bennett was once asked 'Who's the most exciting player you ever played with?' He paused thoughtfully. His answer was about to give those of us gathered around the table good reason to pause and think ourselves.

'Ivor Allchurch,' he said.

Phil, an accomplished soccer player himself, had actually played charity matches with the former Swansea, Newcastle, Cardiff and Wales inside forward. And he went on: 'He was such a balanced runner; he could pivot on a sixpence and still shield the ball from defenders – incredible; a genius!' Praise indeed from a fellow genius.

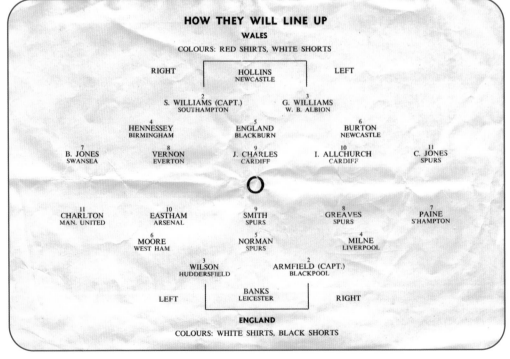

HOW THEY WILL LINE UP

WALES

COLOURS: RED SHIRTS, WHITE SHORTS

RIGHT — HOLLINS NEWCASTLE — LEFT

2 S. WILLIAMS (CAPT.) SOUTHAMPTON — 3 G. WILLIAMS W. B. ALBION

4 HENNESSEY BIRMINGHAM — 5 ENGLAND BLACKBURN — 6 BURTON NEWCASTLE

7 B. JONES SWANSEA — 8 VERNON EVERTON — 9 J. CHARLES CARDIFF — 10 I. ALLCHURCH CARDIFF — 11 C. JONES SPURS

11 CHARLTON MAN. UNITED — 10 EASTHAM ARSENAL — 9 SMITH SPURS — 8 GREAVES SPURS — 7 PAINE S'HAMPTON

6 MOORE WEST HAM — 5 NORMAN SPURS — 4 MILNE LIVERPOOL

3 WILSON HUDDERSFIELD — 2 ARMFIELD (CAPT.) BLACKPOOL

LEFT — BANKS LEICESTER — RIGHT

ENGLAND

COLOURS: WHITE SHIRTS, BLACK SHORTS

Names to conjure with. Wales v England, 1963.

Having received his early education at Plasmarl in Swansea, Ivor Allchurch played his first game for his home-town club at Upton Park on Christmas Day 1949. Throughout the 1950s, he was constantly pursued by such clubs as Arsenal, Spurs and Wolves, all keen to sign the talented Welshman. His fame was also spreading abroad as representatives from two Italian clubs, Bel Bologna and Internazionale, joined the race to secure his signature.

Allchurch, however, refused all of these offers. At Swansea Town, he felt he was part of a large family and was treated as a favourite child. He was given free rein to play his natural game and the only instruction given as he ran onto the field was 'Enjoy yourself!' The instruction given to the other team members must have been, 'Give the ball to Ivor!'

As time moved on, Ivor Allchurch's desire for First Division football overtook his love for Swansea, and on October 10, 1958 he signed for Newcastle United. He had a dream start at his new club, scoring two goals in his first match against Leicester City, but unfortunately his time at Newcastle was not entirely smooth. The club was undergoing a period of restructuring and, with all the attendant problems such times produce, there must have been the odd moment when Allchurch regretted leaving South Wales for the North East of England.

However, he often delighted the fans on the terraces. A report in the *Evening News* after a 4-0 victory against Everton speaks volumes: 'The United fans have never seen Allchurch quite so brilliantly commanding. Long passes to the wings made one gasp with admiration of sheer perfection of "strength". Even Shackleton never entertained more pawkily than did Ivor, as he shuffled the ball across and around a "sixpence" to the bewilderment of three or four challenges.'

Not surprisingly, Ivor Allchurch also made his mark at international level, winning 68 caps for Wales and scoring a total of 24 goals. His greatest hour came in Sweden during the 1958 Football World Cup. Wales were within a whisker of reaching the quarter-final stage and were playing Hungary in a play-off match and Allchurch's goal after 55 minutes was surely the goal of the tournament. A John Charles header was taken on the volley and torpedoed from a distance of 40 yards into the corner of the net. Grosics in the Hungarian goal did not stand a chance. Fifteen minutes from the end, a goal from Terry Medwin secured a Welsh win.

The opponents in the semi-finals were the mighty Brazilians. Unfazed by the occasion or the opposition, the Welsh team again gave a good account of themselves before losing to a single goal. Of course, Allchurch and his team were disappointed but his gloom was lightened somewhat when he was approached by Sēnor Bernabeu, Chairman of Real Madrid. The latter congratulated Ivor on having shown everyone that he was the best inside forward in the world.

Or, as the late Sir Matt Busby, the legendary manager at Manchester United, once said :

> Ivor never needed a number on his back for identification. His polish, his class could not be missed. He vies with the greatest of all time. Yet he has a modesty that becomes him.

The statue of Ivor Allchurch outside the Liberty Stadium in Swansea.

Typically 'magical footwork'.

RYAN GIGGS

'One of the best footballers in the world.' That was Ronaldhino's simple description of Ryan Giggs. Indeed, the Barcelona and Brazil striker has said on more than one occasion that he would gladly pay to stand on the terraces at Old Trafford just to watch him in action.

Giggs's manager at Manchester United for the last fifteen seasons, Sir Alex Ferguson, has many times tried to analyse his player's flair and genius : 'If there is one factor that separates him from other very good players, and gives him a real chance of being truly great, it is his balance. He can wrongfoot anybody just by movement, and when you think a tackler is going to get a foot to the ball, he seems to float or ride over the challenge. The defender always seems to go down while the lad stays on his feet.' Or as Sir Alex once stated in more poetic vein: Giggs in full flight is like 'a dog chasing tin foil in the wind'.

In a recent poll, the goal that Ryan scored against Arsenal in the 1999 FA Cup semi-final at Villa Park was voted the best goal ever scored in the competition. With the match going into extra time, Patrick Vieira dithered on the halfway line. This was enough for Giggs. In a flash he was tearing into the Gunners' half. With three defenders to beat, he successfully outmanoeuvred the first, skilfully maintained possession on his favoured left foot, inviting the remaining two onto the ball. With some magical footwork he completely outwitted the

With David Beckham, former clubmate at Manchester United.

Arsenal defenders. Having reached the box, Martin Keown and Lee Dixon closed in on the Welsh wizard but with a sudden and unexpected change of pace, he left the two defenders paralysed. He then unleashed a left-foot chip of unnerring accuracy which flashed across the goal, dipping under the bar, completely deceiving the experienced David Seaman in the Arsenal goal. It proved the winning goal, a goal made in heaven, in a 2-1 win.

Ryan Giggs considers himself to be Welsh through and through. He was born in Cardiff, as were his parents before him, and he can trace his Welsh

ancestry back through several generations. Indeed, in spite of claims that he would have been better off playing for England, the truth is that he would not have been qualified – or had the inclination to do so. The result is that he has never played in the World Cup finals, but he is one of a quartet of truly world-class players who have been denied that accolade, Alfredo Di Stéfano, George Best and Eric Cantona being the others.

The extent of Ryan Giggs' fame stretches from being the most decorated player in Manchester

United's history to being the only Premiership player to appear on *The Simpsons*. John Hardy, BBC Wales's respected football commentator, reminisces: 'He captained England Schoolboys, but by the time I caught up with him playing for Wales U16s, I witnessed three Englishmen trying, unsuccessfully, to mark him out of the game. An Old Trafford regular once told me that Ryan was so special that supporters with impaired vision would know when he had the ball for a hushed silence would descend over the ground, and ever since his debut at the age of sixteen, the flying left winger has kept football followers on the edge of their seats.'

His international manager Terry Yorath once described him as a genius who could visualise things in slow motion, while everybody else was scurrying around. Ryan was like a downhill skïer analysing each situation at his own pace, 'Like a lot of the greats, he even blinks slowly' was Yorath's assessment.

Amongst all the plaudits, the highest accolade probably comes from another of Wales's legendary players. Kevin Ratcliffe's 59th and last cap for his country coincided with Ryan's first full international and a goal in a 3-1 win against Belgium in 1993. Praise from your peers is praise indeed, but as Ratcliffe pondered his departure from the international scene, he said that the most satisfying part of his career was the fact that he could tell his grandchildren that he played with Ryan Giggs.

Fans pay tribute during his final international match.

JOHN CHARLES

What if? Two short words to concentrate the mind. What if Llywelyn had been victorious at Cilmeri in 1282 – then everyone living east of Offa's Dyke would be natural Welsh speakers. What if Charles Evans had not been taken ill on May 28, 1953 – then a Welshman would have been the first to set foot on the top of Everest.

And, in the quarter-finals of the World Cup in Sweden in 1958, what if one of the best players in the world at the time had not been injured, maybe Wales would have gone on to lift the Jules Rimet trophy. John Charles had been forced to withdraw after some horrific Hungarian tackling in a play-off match. So, Dave Bowen's team had to take the field against Brazil without their talisman – and lost to a solitary goal, Pele's first in World Cup football.

Jack Charlton, one of the heroes of the successful England team of 1966, maintains that John Charles was one of the best players who ever graced a football pitch. A giant on the field, he was also an excellent ambassador off it and everyone who met him agreed that he was a gentleman.

His early days as an apprentice with Swansea Town

saw him endear himself to the staff and fellow players alike. His warm manner, friendly personality and enthusiasm for the game were infectious, and made him a firm favourite at the Vetch. In true fairy-tale fashion, however, it was not at the Vetch that his footballing skills were recognised. Rather he was spotted whilst playing a friendly fixture on a local park by Leeds United scouts who pressed manager, Major Frank Buckley, to sign him immediately.

So it was that in January 1949, John Charles became a Leeds United player. His signing-on fee was £10, and in addition he received a new suit, shirt, tie, shoes and an overcoat. It was not long before Buckley was to be heard boasting of Charles that 'He is the most complete footballer playing the game today.' Two years of National Service followed and when he returned to Leeds, the boy had developed into a man. John Charles was tall, strong and muscular but famously gentle by nature.

He was the finest Welsh footballer since Billy Meredith. He helped Juve to three Serie A Championships and two Italian Cups and scored an amazing 93 goals in 155 league games. In 38 internationals he scored 15 goals, including a hat-trick against Northern Ireland, the second goal of which was, by all reports, sensational. After receiving the ball on the halfway line, he tore through the defence and fired the ball into the upper right-hand corner of the net. 'Unbelievable,' was one headline the following morning.

In his book, *Michael Parkinson on Football*, the writer and broadcaster devotes a whole chapter to the Welsh icon. The title of the piece shows the high esteem in which Parkinson held his hero: 'John Charles was the best centre-half in the world as well as the best centre-forward.' At home in both positions, he had the balance of a gymnast and the speed of an Olympic athlete.

In a career which spanned fifteen years, John Charles's disciplinary conduct was exemplary. His name was never written into the referee's notebook, he was never warned for dissent. He totally ignored those players who set out to intimidate him – he had his own standards of behaviour and stuck to them rigidly. An example of John Charles's gentlemanly conduct was illustrated in a local derby played between Juventus and Torino. During an attacking movement, close to the Turin goal, he accidentally floored one of the opposing defenders. Instead of taking advantage and shooting for goal, he kicked the ball towards the touchline and ran towards the injured player. Both sets of supporters looked on in disbelief. You can just imagine what Wenger, Ferguson or Mourhino would have told him!

To quote Daley Thompson, Stewart Binns and Tom Lewis in *The Greatest*: 'John Charles is living proof that sometimes nice guys do finish first. Everything you read about the man, even from opponents, testifies to what a nice man he was, even while playing!'

'*Il Buon Gigante*' indeed – one of football's favourite sons.

'Don't pick it up, Gareth!' From left to right, Ivor Allchurch, Gareth Edwards and John Charles in a charity match.

TANNI GREY-THOMPSON

Seoul 1988, Barcelona 1992, Atlanta 1996, Sydney 2000 ... No, it is not a quiz question demanding that you name the next venue, but a roll-call of all the Olympic Games in which Tanni Grey-Thompson has taken part – and returned home victorious. A feat which has made her one of the best athletes in the world.

Small wonder, therefore, that the British Paralympic team of 2004 looked to her for inspiration as their captain as the Athens games approached. No one doubted Tanni's enthusiasm and commitment to the cause despite the fact that some felt that she was now coming to the end of what had been a glittering career. Things started badly, however, when she failed miserably in the 800m final. As soon as the race was over, the commentators pounced. The BBC's Paul Dickinson, who was always supportive of Tanni, pulled no punches when he posed the question 'A games too far for Tanni?'

She herself was appalled with her performance and accepted that she had been guilty of some bad tactical errors. She came in a disappointing seventh, her worst-ever Paralympic

A family celebration in Athens.

placement. In a competitive and often cut-throat environment, some were quite happy Tanni hadn't won whilst others were supportive and genuinely wanted to get her back on track. It was all hard to deal with. She prided herself on 100% performances and was physically drained and emotionally upset at the end of the race. The BBC in their usual manner were present at the finish with the interviewer Phil Jones in apologetic mood stating 'We'll speak to you later.' 'No, we'll do it now,' was the immediate reply. His questions were challenging, and Tanni had to admit to her own inadequacies on the day. As she remarked afterwards, 'If you want media coverage when you win, then you must be prepared to be confronted, often quite brutally, when you lose.'

With the interviews at an end, Tanni made her way track side where her emotions took over. After several episodes of vomiting and crying in turn, she eventually managed to regain her composure and make her way to where her daughter Cerys was being looked after by her great friends Maureen and Ray Loughran. Ray's greeting was typically forthright, 'Tanni, you underperformed. You can do better!' This was just what she needed to hear – an honest opinion from a trusted friend and the impetus required to focus both physically and mentally on the next race, the 100 metres. Cerys on the other hand was completely nonplussed. 'Did you see mummy race?' was the question asked. The answer was a little unexpected, if understandable. 'No, I was eating a hot dog!'

One of Tanni's closest friends, Jenny Ridley and her coach Jason Bridges were unbelievably supportive. Jenny was a fellow competitor who couldn't race in Athens because of an administrative technicality. It was, therefore, an emotionally traumatic time for her but she enthusiastically supported her colleague. She even went training with Tanni in preparation for the 100m providing the under-pressure athlete with loads of confidence.

The 100 metres was the weakest event in Tanni's repertoire. In preparation for the event, she pored over her training diary, listing the races she had won over the distance and trying to re-live the experience. This was an attempt to psyche herself up for the forthcoming challenge. A difficult decision was to say to her husband Ian, one of the team's coaches, 'I want you around. I want to know you're there, but I don't want you as coach for the 100 metres.' Ian accepted this decision with good grace.

This race developed into one of the most important of Tanni's career. It was a hot, dry, sunny Athens morning but she turned up at the stadium some four hours before the start of the event. With a huge umbrella to provide shelter and enough water to embark on a crossing of the Sahara Desert, she began making her preparations. While the intent was good, the execution left a lot to be desired. Tanni was so nervous that she could not stop shaking. This coupled with repeated bouts of vomiting meant that she could only push a lap at a time as opposed to her usual routine of six to ten kilometre warm-up. If she wasn't vomiting then her continuous retching meant that her coach Jason had to apply bags of ice to her neck to try and relieve some of the tension and anxiety in her body. Tanni had decided to have her hair cut short for these games so when Jason remarked 'At least I don't have to hold your hair back when you're sick!', a semblance of a smile was brought to her face, the first of the day!

With the start of the race fast approaching, the Welsh athlete felt that it was now or never for salvaging her career. Her preparations had not been what she had hoped for and her acceleration skills still needed fine tuning – she was so nervous her hands would not stop shaking. And then a pivotal moment. Her friend, fellow competitor and great rival Francesca Portellato approached. 'Are you OK?' she asked. 'Not really,' was the honest reply. 'I had such a poor 800 metres.' Concerned at her friend's obvious distress, the Italian athlete added, 'You'll be fine for the hundred. You don't look too happy, but you should be. You're the best in the world and you're going to win!'

With her confidence at its lowest ebb, this was exactly what Tanni needed to hear..

'On your marks,' the starter's voice boomed and after what seemed an eternity, they were off. Francesca who was two lanes away to Tanni's left shot off the starting line, while Tanni could not get her rhythm going at all. However, at 40 metres, with everything falling into place nicely, she overtook her opponent and with what seemed very little effort crossed the finishing line first. The Italian came in second, followed by the American, Miriam Nibley, who had fancied her chances for the gold after Tanni's disastrous 800 metres.

Once the race was over, as she was mobbed by friends, administrators and fellow athletes alike, Tanni suffered a small degree of anticlimax. She looked and felt miserable; there was no sense of elation, just relief that she had won. A newspaper picture on the following morning showed Tanni's husband Ian looking in another direction as she passed the 35-metre mark. 'Why weren't you watching?' she asked.

'I knew you'd won,' came the reply. In a typical understatement Tanni confirmed that this was possibly the most romantic thing her husband had ever said to her! Thankfully her daughter had watched her mother race this time, but as a reward felt that she now deserved an ice cream!

It was a partcularly emotional reunion with Ian, Jenny and Jason – her three most trusted friends and confidants. Even when she had been near to despair, they had believed in her and now she was able to live up to their expectations.

After coming a disappointing fourth in the 200 metres, Tanni had one more event left where she could gain a medal to become Britain's most prolific medallist in the Paralympics. The 400-metre final was to be broadcast live on breakfast television in Britain. The build-up to the final had been intense and previewed daily, and Tanni had been forewarned that Clare Balding and Colin Jackson would be at the finishing line waiting to interview her.

In Commonwealth Games action, 2006.

She won the race comfortably, was on a high and grinning broadly from ear to ear. As the two commentators approached and asked in unison 'How do you feel?', Tanni's immediate reply was, 'So glad I didn't get you two out of bed for nothing!' Such repartee with colleagues has always proved endearing to all those who come into contact with Tanni and this makes her such a firm favourite with broadcasters, the press and fans alike.

Her lack of pretension is also illustrated in the story she tells of her first meeting with the great Gareth Edwards. It was during the Welsh Sports Personality of the Year award ceremony in Cardiff during the early 1990s. The former scrum half introduced himself: 'Hi, I'm Gareth Edwards.' 'I know. I remember watching you play when I was little — you were my hero,' she replied. He certainly had an impact on Tanni's career, and those victories in Athens would likewise have made an impact on him.

JIMMY WILDE

Welsh boxers are a breed apart. And to choose between them is to incur the wrath of that most robustly discerning of sports supporters, the Welsh boxing fan.

I have chosen to tread carefully, therefore, preferring to upset the likes of Hugh McIlvanney than to make ill-educated claims about the pugilistic heroes of Wales. McIlvanney, the highly respected football correspondent, is critical of those journalists who cannot function unless fuelled by quotes. He highlights their inadequacies, their insistence on allowing managers and players to interpret the action for them.

But quotes are essential if I am to do justice to Jimmy Wilde. Likewise to Freddie Welsh. In fact, I have had to rely heavily on the opinions of a host of experts in this respect, because choosing only two boxers from such an illustrious list was a task beyond my limited appreciation of this the darkest and most romanticized of all sports.

Those experts were eloquent in their assessment of the likes of Percy Jones, Jim Driscoll, Tommy Farr, Eddie Thomas, Joe Erskine, Dick Richardson, Dai Dower, Howard Winstone, Colin Jones, Brian Curvis, Johnny Owen and Joe Calzaghe. But, time and again, at the top of this list, were placed the names of Wilde and Welsh. And it's then that I started to need those quotes.

I asked a personal friend and boxing aficionado R. Maldwyn Thomas to compose a piece on Wilde's World Championship fight with the 'Young Zulu Kid', an Italian-American named Guiseppe di Mefi whose nickname derived from the golliwog he always carried as a mascot.

'It is the week before Christmas. Thick fog surrounds Holborn Stadium in London. Lamps had been lit since the early afternoon. The metallic sounds of trams on their tracks, the sound of horses' hooves, the sound of thousands of feet on the street. Men with cloth caps and mufflers. The smell of beer and cigarettes. Busy bookies from Bermondsey and Bow. The rich Jews of Golders Green, coats with astrakhan collars. The smell of cigars. Soldiers from the trenches of Flanders in khaki.

In the bowels of the stadium, the Welshman is the irritable Jimmy Wilde; a thin, pale boxer, five feet and three inches tall. He was to have fought at two o'clock in the afternoon. It's now a quarter to four. White tiles, buckets, the smell of sweat, blood and ointment. The previous bout has just finished. He's climbing the stairs lightfootedly with Teddy Lewis, his manager, carrying his small bag.

The thousands in Holborn are screaming. Jimmy Wilde is the hero. Everyone wants to see the amazing little Welshman .

"My Lords! Gentlemen! The bout for the World Flyweight Championship! Weighing seven stone ten pounds, Featherweight champion of Great Britain!

European Champion! And the World Flyweight Champion! From Tylorstown, Glamorganshire – Jimmy Wilde!"

And there's the "Young Zulu Kid" from America in the other corner. He's shorter than Jimmy Wilde, five feet, but strong, stocky. He's very confident. And America acclaims him as the true champion. The afternoon's event will decide. The two are ready. The first round and the Kid is keeping close to Jimmy. Punches to the stomach. But Jimmy's arms are never-ending, like long knives. Jimmy dancing and the Kid looking clumsy. Round Two, and Jimmy hits the stomach and the head. The Kid hits the canvas. A count starts but the bell saves him.

Eighteen more rounds according to the programme. Round Three and Jimmy is as hard as ever. He was working in a pit in the Rhondda at the age of nine. Jimmy's fists are an insane kaleidoscope. The Kid is stubborn and hard. Round Six... Round Nine. And the Kid is pressing the Welshman's ribs. But he's sluggish. And Jimmy is mercurial.

Round Eleven and the thousands inside the Stadium foresee the inevitable. To the left, to the right, up and down. And Jimmy improving with every round. The long steel arms. Hitting, spearing, flowing and hitting again. The Kid is on the canvas. The hurrahs rise in chords from bench to bench, from row to row, from floor to ceiling. The Kid looks pitiful, his confidence in the spit bucket. And Jimmy leaves the ring as lighfootedly as he had entered. Teddy Lewis had no reason to open the little bag once during the bout.'

The last word, however, goes to Nat Fleischer, the American editor of the magazine *The Ring* who constantly reminded the boxing public of the incredible bravery of Welsh boxers. He was a compulsive compiler of lists and on top of his best ever flyweights there was only ever one name: Jimmy Wilde.

Joe Calzaghe.

FREDDIE WELSH

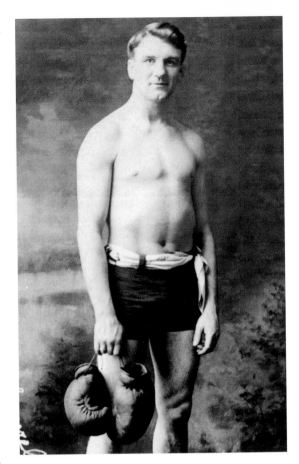

The Great Gatsby was Welsh. And if I hadn't read Andrew Gallimore's book *Occupation Prizefighter : The Freddie Welsh Story*, I would still be unaware that the hero of F. Scott Fitzgerald's novel was actually modelled on Frederick Hall Thomas of Morgan Sreet, Pontypridd. Or rather, Freddie Welsh as he was known in the USA.

He was a champion boxer whose grandfather, Morgan Thomas, was a bare-knuckle fighter of some repute at a time when such bouts took place atop some remote mountain range far away from the prying eyes of the authorities. The industrial valleys of South Wales with their rows of terraced houses clinging limpet-like to the steep sides of the valley proved to be a fertile breeding ground for boxers during the early part of the twentieth century. Such was the poverty that earning a few pounds for going a few rounds in the ring was seen as an escape from the drudgery of day-to-day life.

Ironically, Freddie Welsh was born into a wealthy family and sent at an early age to a prestigious boarding school in Bristol, but his time there was not a happy one. Ultimately he abandoned an academic career and announced that he wanted to become an engineer. However, and in an era when gap years were a phenomenon of the future, he subsequently decided to take time out from his apprenticeship to travel around North America. At the age of seventeen, he eventually took up residency in the United States and embarked upon a boxing career that would take him from coast to coast.

Freddie Welsh was born to box. He was certainly the best of his generation, some would argue the best ever. Light of foot, his balance was impeccable, and he had a left hand which was as accurate and potent as an engine piston. Boxing has been described as the art of self-defence – if so, Freddie was the finest exponent of all time. He himself bore no marks of his craft, such was his skill at avoiding punches from bemused opponents.

While most of his career was spent abroad, Freddie did manage a few bouts in Britain. The most notable was his challenge for the World Lightweight title at the Olympia Theatre in London on July 7, 1914. Ten thousand tickets were sold, ranging in price from five shillings to ten guineas for a ringside seat. The evening was unique in that it was the first time that women were allowed into a boxing

Two Welsh boxers who came close to world-title glory, Johnny Owen and Colin Jones.

could offer. He was however, always on hand to help out a friend in need, and also became a patron of the arts and a supporter of good causes. It was during this period that the friendship with F. Scott Fitzgerald developed. The two were often seen exercising together, or discussing the works of Tolstoy or Maeterlinck.

Unfortunately, with the Great Depression causing huge financial problems across the country, Welsh too found himself in dire financial straits and his life took a tragically downward spiral. Frederick Hall Thomas died penniless in a hotel in Hell's Kitchen.

In its tribute to one of the all-time greats, The Ring reminded boxing fans the world over not only of Freddie Welsh's genius and artistry, but also of life's vagaries: 'Such is the way of the world! One day a hero, with millions of worshippers at your door; the next, a down-and-outer with none to offer succor!'

match – and they were there in their thousands. True to form, Freddie insisted that the contest be staged on a Saturday night to enable miners from the valleys to attend.

The fight would be decided over twenty rounds. Many thought that Welsh's artistry and skill would carry him through, others favoured the holder Ritchie's superior strength and power. In the end there was no real contest – the Welshman won by a huge margin, not one dissenting voice was raised in protest at the decision of the referee, Eugene Corri as he raised Freddie Welsh's arm as the victor. Strains of 'Hen Wlad Fy Nhadau' could be heard around Covent Garden into the small hours.

Freddie Welsh became a rich man as a result of his success, and, along with his wife Brahna and their two children, enjoyed all the trappings that wealth

A riot in the ring after Welsh's defeat of Jim Driscoll, 1920.

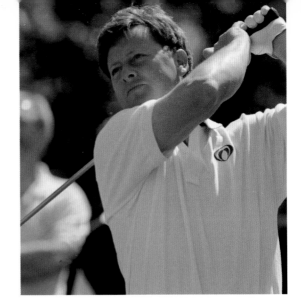

IAN WOOSNAM

It is 1991, and at the US Masters in Augusta, the great Tom Watson is being willed on to victory by the hugely partisan American supporters.

His opponent, on the other hand, is the object of spiteful derision. If he mistimes a putt, they cheer; if he drives into the rough or a bunker, they ridicule his effort. Like Manchester United's Ronaldo,

taunted and abused at all grounds in the Premiership, Watson's rival is given a torrid time. Things get so bad that Watson apologises to him for the crowd's behaviour.

But like Ronaldo, he buckles down, blocks out the jibes and battles on bravely. He is Ian Woosnam and with one hole left to play, he is, against all odds, one stroke ahead.

Such was the situation when the diminutive Welshman's drive landed clear of the bunker but left him out of sight of the flag. It took all the authority the marshalls could muster to clear the crowd and carve an opening for his second shot. Miraculously, it reached the lip of the green. By some stroke of fate, Tom Watson's second shot landed in sand just off the green. In reality both players were in a lot of trouble.

From the sand, Watson's third shot splashed 25 feet past the pin whilst Woosnam putted admirably to within seven feet. Watson's downhill putt rolled five feet past. Seven feet thus separated Woosnam from immortality. Confidently he stroked the ball and immediately knew it was in. 'Perhaps,' he said afterwards, 'they'll now be able to say my name right. Maybe even spell it correctly.'

His mischievous sense of humour is well documented and never better demonstrated than

1993 Ryder Cup, with Bernhard Langer (left) and caddie.

at Augusta a year after his remarkable triumph. Tickets at the United States Masters are hard to come by. They're usually handed down from generation to generation, and plastic card accreditation is required to gain entry into the VIP enclosure and the plush clubhouse. So imagine Sir Stan Thomas, Ian Botham and Max Boyce's situation as they travelled to Georgia to support their bosom pal.

Woosie's family (who were entitled to special tickets and privileges) decided to stay at home so Ian duly sent by courier some items (originally intended for his wife and daughters) to the hotel where his three intrepid mates were staying. When they eventually arrived at the Augusta National, they encountered security checks on a par with the arrivals hall at Ben Gurion airport, Tel Aviv and, upon approaching the main gate for VIPs, they were stopped and interrogated thus :

'ID, Sir?' quizzed an officious-looking security guard. Max Boyce pointed proudly to the plastic card hanging loosely around his neck. He half expected to be allowed immediate entry but was stopped in his tracks. The questioning continued: 'Is that your name Sir – Amy Woosnam?'

'It is,' he replied with a measure of conviction and embarassment. 'It's a very popular Christian name for men in South Wales.'

'Can you confirm, Sir, that your friend's name is Amy Woosnam?' the official asked Sir Stan, who was next in line and breathing heavily.

'I certainly can,' he said, who now had to convince the cautious American that his name was Rebecca! But the magical moment was to hear Ian Botham, one of the most famous cricketers in the history of the game – Alexander the Great, Roy of the Rovers and Bruce Willis rolled into one – state categorically that his name was Glendryth Woosnam! What would Sir Vivian Richards have said?

For all his playfulness, on the golf course his uncanny judgement and consistency resulted in successes at major tournaments, where his timing and metronomic swing were admired worldwide. His preparations were always meticulous but it was his courage and willpower that often proved decisive. As Lee Trevino said, 'They'll never bury Woosie because they'll never get his heart into the coffin!'

Holding the 2002 Ryder Cup with fellow Welsh golfer, Philip Price.

Dai Rees, so close to winning a major.

He now lives in Jersey and recently stated that the proudest triumph of his career was captaining Europe to Ryder Cup Glory at the K Club in 2006. But I can't help remembering that last round in Augusta. Two other outstanding Welsh golfers, namely Dai Rees and Dave Thomas had come close to winning a Major, but Woosie actually did it. And it was all the sweeter for having happened on American soil.

DAVID DAVIES

How is it that one instictively wakes seconds before the alarm sounds to shatter the still of the night? This is a question that must have been asked a thousand times in the Davies household in Barry as each parent took it in turn to get the youngster out of his bed and onto the road to Cardiff for an early morning training session.

These sessions usually started at 6am and lasted for some two hours. After a hasty shower, a breakfast (lovingly prepared by his mother the previous evening) and a change into his school uniform, it was then a mad dash to St Cyres School in Penarth for the first of the day's lessons. When the bell rang at the end of the day, the routine would be reversed and it would be a race back to Sophia Gardens for the evening coaching session. This was a typical day in the life of a would-be Olympian.

Though David Davies was first introduced to the swimming pool at the tender age of five when he was taken to the leisure centre at Barry, it was not until he was sixteen years of age that he was taken under the wing of knowledgeable coach Dave Haller. And, following the

Martin Woodroffe,
Wales's Olympic silver-medallist in 1968.

British Championships in 2001, he won a bronze medal at the European Youth Championships in Murcia in Spain. 2002 saw him represent Wales at the Commonwealth Games in Manchester where he reached the final of the 1500m individual medley. With enough hard work, it was thought, he could emulate the success enjoyed by Paul Radmilovic, Valerie Davies and Martyn Woodroffe and win Olympic pool medals.

And, to this end, David applied himself. Consequently, his weekly schedule is one that would tax Superman, Bruce Willis and Arnold Schwarzenegger and even cause some trepidation amongst the ranks of the New Zealand All Blacks. Can you imagine what swimming the equivalent of 50 miles every week does to your body?

When he arrived at the Athens Olympic Games in 2004, he felt fitter than he had ever been, both mentally and physically. What is more, he achieved his first aim: he reached the final of the 1500m freestyle. Here he would be up against sporting giants, including two of the world's best in Grant Hackett of Australia and Larsen Jensen of the United States. The press and media were concentrating their attentions on the rivalry between these two. As far as they were concerned, David Davies was just one of the new kids on the block. Dave Haller, however, was quietly confident that his protege would hold his own in such illustrious company

With the scene now set for the final, the tension around the pool was palpable, spectators and officials alike almost afraid to draw breath. David's parents, sitting in the stands, were conscious that everyone could hear their hearts pounding. Once the buzzer sounded, Grant Hackett took off like a torpedo, hotly pursued by Jensen and young David Davies. With only 400m remaining, the Welshman was incredibly in second place and it was only thanks to a superhuman effort by the American that David Davies was denied a silver medal. However, the nineteen-year-old Welshman had smashed the British and European record, clocking 14.45.95 and knocking a massive twelve seconds off his personal best.

David Davies has already achieved so much (his latest gold was at the Commonwealth Games at Melbourne in 2006) but his aim once his swimming days are over is to follow an academic path. Whatever his future plans, this personable, well-mannered young man will make his mark. A role model for the younger generation, he is an excellent ambassador for sport in general.

Ecstatic and disbelieving, David embraced his fellow competitors, However, minutes later, when he was interviewed poolside by Sharon Davies, his reaction was typically self-effacing, 'Chill out Sharon – calm down for goodness' sake!' he said in front of millions of viewers back home.

But, at present, hopes are high that he will emulate that other Davies (Lynn) and bring another individual Olympic Gold Medal to Wales. Can you imagine how many budding young swimmers will be in the water in Barry Island?

COLIN JACKSON

Lists often tell us nothing. The following one, I promise, is an exception:

Three silver medals and one gold medal at the World Indoor Championships. One silver and two golds at the European Indoor Indoor Championships. Two Commonwealth silvers, and two Commonwealth golds. Four European Championship gold medals. One bronze, one silver and two golds at the World Championships. One Olympic Games silver. (Oh, and by the way, two 110m hurdles world records.)

It is a list that makes you wonder where Colin Jackson finds room in his house to keep the Rice Krispies and DVDs.

It says a lot about this country of ours that many people's abiding image of Colin Jackson is of him being denied a richly-deserved Olympic title in 1992 as he hit those hurdles in Barcelona – or his appearances on *Strictly Come Dancing* even! Yet his was a sporting dynasty as long-lived as Manchester United's in football, the Chicago Bulls in basketball and Stade Toulousain in rugby football. He was feared and respected by his fellow athletes, and made stars like Allen Johnson and Florian Schwarzkopf wish they'd been born in a different era.

Colin Jackson attended Llanedeyrn High School in Cardiff. A sporting all-rounder, he would soon be taken under the wing of coach Malcolm Arnold and transformed into an excellent hurdler and long jumper. He announced his presence on the world stage, however, by winning silver at the Seoul Olympics in 1998, and was undeniably (and justifiably) favourite for Olympic gold at Barcelona four years later. Many variables, ranging from a suspicion of a hidden injury and the sheer weight of a nation's expectation on his shoulders, contributed to his disappointing seventh place that day. However, as the former heavyweight boxer Floyd Patterson claimed, the measure of a sportsman is not how he gets knocked down but how he gets back up.

And, at the World Championships at Stuttgart in 1993, how Jackson got up! Indeed that fateful Barcelona day may well have inspired his running of the fastest 110-metre hurdles race in history. Jack Pierce of the USA and Englishman Tony Jarrett shared the podium with Jackson that night, but they would be the first to admit that they were there as the proverbial also-rans. He blasted out of the blocks (he was rumoured to be quicker than even Linford Christie over the first 30m of a 100m) and, with that combination of subtlety and grace over the hurdles and raw power on the floor, simply ran away from the field. Had he not been a true professional and perfectionist, he could theoretically have started preparing his victory lap after the third hurdle. As soon as he threw himself over the line with that single-fingered salute and scream of exhilaration, a thousand posters in a thousand sports centres around Britain were born. Symbolically, in exchanging gloom at Barca for joy in Germany, he went from being Colin the Welshman to Colin the Brit.

Becoming world champion in a near-perfect exhibition of sprint hurdling meant that Jackson had regained his persona. He went from being the athlete whom most mothers would like to *cwtsh* and console after Barcelona to being the ruthless winner whom we all cheered from one win to the next, rejoicing, as Welshmen, that that man was 'one of ours'.

He would win the world title again in 1999 but it would be that first world-record-breaking win that would define Colin Jackson's career. The world best of 12.91 seconds was equalled by Liu Xiang in the 2004 Summer Olympics, and finally beaten by the same man in 2006 with a time of 12.88. To date Jackson still holds the indoor world record of 7.30 seconds, a time, it would seem, that even a seven-foot Chinaman cannot yet touch.

Jackson has been awarded both the MBE and CBE for services to athletics, and those services now include coaching Rhys Williams, one of the best quarter-mile runners in the world. Both are also Welsh and would have grown up admiring and wanting to emulate their esteemed coach. It would be very satisfying should Jackson the coach achieve the Olympic gold that Jackson the athlete missed out on.

The proud Welshman celebrates.

Lynn Davies

It was the summer of 1961, and the first Friday in May. At Ogmore Grammar the usual preparations were being made for the school's annual (and short-lived) date with athletics. It was Sports Day!

The council ten-ton tipper lorry would, of course, have made its customary pilgrimage from the depot to the school field to fill a hole with sand and gravel for the long jump pit, little knowing that it had been setting the stage for an event of international significance.

With a leap of 21 feet that day, the 1961 senior long jump champion at Ogmore Grammar School was one Lynn Davies from Nantymoel. Had 21st-century technology been available at the time, the sports master, Royden Thomas, would have called for the third umpire or a video replay such was his astonishment. His gymnastic tuition may well have been crucial to the young athlete's overall development, but he had never foreseen this!

Within a week, Lynn was representing the school at the county sports at Maindee Stadium in Cardiff where he once again reigned supreme. As fate would have it, a new Welsh National Athletics coach had just been appointed, and when Ron Pickering witnessed Davies's jump of 22 feet, he was genuinely excited. He immediately realised that here was a future star in the making.

Over the next three years, with Lynn by now a student at Cardiff Training College, a special understanding and relationship developed between mentor and pupil. Ron, lively and charismatic, was also a perfectionist. He believed in meticulous preparation coupled with the dogma that speed, strength and technique were imperative to achieve success as a long jumper. In Lynn he had an eager pupil, one who was willing to listen, keen to learn and hungry for success.

Within eighteen months, during the 1962 season, Lynn was seen wearing the red vest of Wales in the British and Empire Commonwealth Games in Perth, Australia. With a jump of 25 feet in the final round, he came an impressive fourth. Disappointed at not getting a medal, he nevertheless realised that this experience could only stand him in good stead for future championshps.

Taking part in Perth also proved to be a bizarre experience for the young Welshman in another way. He found himself sharing a room in the athlete's village with John Merriman, winner of the silver medal in the six-mile race at Cardiff. Only four years earlier Lynn had waited patiently on Westgate Street in order to get the his room mate's autograph!

The 1962-63 season saw a period of intense training. Pickering was now concentrating on the Welshman's speed and upper body strength. Long sessions on the track were interspersed with hours in the gym lifting weights and following other rigid disciplines. All this hard work was rewarded when Lynn broke the Commonwealth record at the Inter Counties Championships at the White City in London with a leap of over 26 feet. He also recorded 9.5 seconds for the 100 yards. Fellow athletes were now starting to sit up and take note of Davies's potential – some with admiration, and others with a degree of trepidation.

It was not long before an invitation to join the Olympic squad for the 1964 Tokyo games was pushed through the letter-box at the family home. Whilst it was the talk of the

village that one from their midst would be travelling halfway around the world to represent his country, both mentor and pupil remained focussed on the job in hand. Both were convinced that with continuing hard work and a degree of luck, Lynn Davies would make it to the final round of the long jump competition.

To put all of this in perspective, only four years earlier in 1960, when Ralph Boston, the reigning Olympic champion was collecting his gold medal in Rome, Lynn was standing in a field in the Ogmore valley waiting for the council lorry to arrive!

The journey to Japan was the proverbial nightmare. These were the days when BOAC ruled the skies and there was no immediate long haul flights. Consequently, there were stop-overs at Rome, Tehran, Karachi, Calcutta, and Hong Kong before finally arriving exhausted at Tokyo. It needed a period of almost two weeks to overcome the ensuing jet-lag, but the facilities on offer were state of the art and the food out of this world, especially the king prawns – such delicacies were unheard of in Peglers in Nantymoel.

At the games, the British team got off to a dream start: Mary Rand won the gold medal in the women's long jump, breaking the world record in the process. If the team needed any encouragement to perform then this was exactly what was required.

But what of Lynn? What was going through his mind day by day? With no mobile or e-mail to keep his family back home abreast of developments, his best bet might have been the odd telegram. And, who knows that some of them might not have read as follows?

Closing in on D-day! Tossing and turning. Sub-conscious full of images from past Olympics. Clear blue skies... sweltering sun. Spectators sheltering under kaleidoscopic umbrellas. Alarm rings at 6am. Disaster... torrential rain, gale force winds. Think Nantymoel in February! Pack clothing into kit-bag. Bus leaves promptly at 8am. Qualifying Round starts at 10am. Need to jump 7.80m to reach final. Three attempts. Conditions atrocious. Have to run into eye of storm.

Two no-jumps! Devastated. Ralph Boston, qualifies with ease. Produces a wry smile. Just stand there. Concentrate. Thoughts of dunes at Merthyr Mawr. Hours spent lifting weights. Family pride. Three no-jumps – 'No way!' Fly down the runway. Think of Japan's new bullet train. Five vital seconds. Ron's words... 'Essence of competition – controlled aggression'. Hit the board beautifully. Immediate confirmation. Satisfy judges. Second-best jump of competition.

Showered. Light lunch. Final in two hours. 'You're one of the strongest there!' says coach. Runway soft; drive through the elements. Ron's last words – 'You can get bronze!'

Size-up favourites. Boston and Ter-Ovanesyan in last twelve – athletic icons. Two world champions! 'Winner stakes all!' Weather still diabolical. Colourful umbrellas illuminate grey afternoon. Twelve contest final. Three jumps each; best eight get extra three attempts. Third after three jumps. Distance of no consequence; conditions worsening. Sheltering in dug-out under woolly blankets. Sense Boston is worried. Says, 'No-one will jump 8m today!' They're beatable!

Two jumps left. Can hardly stand up in the wind.

Running speed essential. Looked at stadium flags. Hope. Wind dropped slightly. Went for it! Hit the board. Skipped out of pit. Glanced at scoreboard. Aeons later, as bright as West End theatre lights, a confirmation. 8.07m! Ahead in 5th round. Others psychologically scarred. Boston's last jump. Mustn't underestimate him. Magnificent competitor. Sat back near dug-out; towel on head. Final jump 8.03m. Insufficient. Igor still left. Russian thwarted by sloppy landing. Lynn Davies from Nantymoel – Olympic gold medallist. Unbelievable!

Everyone back home in Wales was bursting with pride as Lord Burghley (himself a gold medallist in the 400m hurdles in Paris in 1924) hung the gold medal around his neck. This was the first time in 68 years that a Welshman had won gold in an individual event in the Olympic Games – and we're still waiting for a second! Lynn Davies of 14, Commercial Street, Nantymoel had now entered the sporting hall of fame.

Following a few celebratory sakis in downtown Shinjuku, Ron and Lyn were up early on the morning following the competition, eager to contact respective families back in Wales. As they entered the post office in the Olympic village, Ralph Boston was seen to be leaving. As he approached the door, a young Welshman proffered his autograph book. 'I think I've seen enough bloody Welshmen for one week,' was Boston's retort.

Telegrams rained down in their thousands on Nantymoel in the days following Lynn's incredible achievement. When he and Ron arrived home, the concourse at Cardiff Central Station was jammed full of excited fans eager to catch a glimpse of a superstar. The council had laid on the mayoral car to transport the duo and Meriel, Lynn's fiancée, back to the family home. All along the route, bunting was strewn across the roads and whole communities had turned out to cheer his arrival. Such was the crush that Lynn had to address the crowd from the open window of his bedroom. In his speech, he thanked everyone for their support – his family, his coach and especially the council workers from Ogmore and Garw Rural District Council who annually filled in the pit!

ACKNOWLEDGEMENTS

The author and publishers gratefully acknowledge the following sources of images:

BBC: p. 1, 15, 23, 27, 32; Western Mail: p. 2, 4, 18; Colorsport: 2, 3, 9, 14, 20, 30, 31, 36, 39; South Wales Evening Post: 7, 16, 29; Jim Gittings: 8; Huw Evans Agency: 8, 9, 10, 11, 12, 13, 19, 30, 33, 34; Glamorgan County Cricket Club: 10; Getty Images: 11, 25, 32, 35; Guardian News & Media Ltd. 2007: 13; Steve Benbow and PhotolibraryWales: 17, 18, 19; Ray Daniel: 21; Tanni Grey-Thompson and Creative Excellence: 22; Mark Lewis: 24, 25; johnnyowen.com: 26, 29; Andrew Gallymore: 28; National Library Wales: 29; Carmarthenshire Archive Service: 36; Press Association: 29, 37.; Audrey Woodroffe: 32.

f/cover: Colorsport/Getty Images

b/cover: BBC/Huw Evans Agency

It has not been possible to trace the owner of copyright in every case. The publishers apologise for any omission and will be pleased to remedy any oversight when re-printing.